CORVETTE
THE COMPLETE
ILLUSTRATED HISTORY

By Jim Campisano

Designed by Matthew Blitz

This edition published in 1992 by SMITHMARK Publishers, Inc.,
112 Madison Avenue, New York, NY 10016.

SMITHMARK Books are available for bulk purchase for sales promotion
and premium use. For details, write or telephone the Manager of Special
Sales, SMITHMARK Publishers, Inc., 112 Madison Avenue, New York,
NY 10016 (212) 532-6600.

© 1992 Platinum Press, Inc.,
311 Crossways Park Drive, Woodbury, NY 11797

ISBN 0-8317-9117-9

Printed in Hong Kong

Contents

I would like to dedicate this book to my parents, Joseph and Florence, for about a million different reasons, but mostly for their support, love and encouragement. Special thanks to Zora Arkus-Duntov, for making the Corvette the best, and never settling for anything less. And to D. Randy Riggs, Editor-in-chief of VETTE magazine, for his assistance with this book and for giving me the chance to write about Corvettes in the first place.

Introduction

Every company, whether it produces cars, magazines, cameras or televisions, must have its "flagship"—a vehicle or device where its best, brightest and newest ideas show up first. A flagship is a company's billboard, its most important advertisement. It screams: "This is what we can do. We're number one. Let's see the competition top this!"

Nowhere is that concept more important, more prevalent, than in the automobile business. When your product represents the second-largest investment most consumers will ever make, it takes more than fancy slogans and scantily clad models to be successful. There must be a commitment to excellence and quality—either real or perceived—that your customers can see. If they can't afford the finest vehicle you build, they at least like to think some of what is in that car has rubbed off or filtered down into the one for which they just shelled out a half-year's income.

For almost 40 years, the Corvette has been the flagship for the Chevrolet Division of General Motors. In fact, one would not be out of line to say that the Corvette is the flagship for the entire GM corporation.

Though the Corvette has never sold in large numbers (by Detroit standards), and as of this writing Chevy still has not produced one million units over the course of 38 years, one can be sure that Chevrolet has sold millions of automobiles in that time because of its two-seater sports car. Chevrolet general manager Jim Perkins likes to say, "There is a little Corvette in every car we build."

That is the role of the flagship.

Every major development from fiberglass bodies and fuel injection to four-wheel disc brakes appeared first on the Vette. Sure, you could get a fuel-injected engine in a Chevy passenger car in 1957 (Pontiacs, too), but it disappeared after only a couple of years. In 1965, it took well over 400 cubic inches from the competition to come close to matching the performance of the "fuelie" Vette. It was truly a legend in its own time.

Cadillac, once the standard of the world, came to symbolize everything that was wrong with the American car industry. It wasn't until lately that it has begun to reverse its fortunes. Time will tell if it is too late or not. Chances are, though, that it will never again be called "the standard of the world."

Only the Corvette has managed to hang in there. When the latest generation debuted in March of 1983 as an '84 model, it was the most advanced production automobile on the planet. Today, from the base Corvette all the way up to the omnipotent 32-valve ZR-1s and Callaway Twin Turbos, the plastic Chevy still boasts of technology far beyond ordinary (and even some extraordinary) cars.

It remains the flagship of the American fleet, a position it holds with pride, dignity and honor. The advances that have appeared on the '92—traction control, asymmetrical tires and a 300-horsepower Generation II small-block V8 that revives the LT-1 name—indicate that General Motors is not about to allow the Corvette to abdicate its throne.

Thank goodness. America needs more cars like the Corvette.

Chapter One

From Small Things, Big Things One Day Come

The sound of a straight Six at speed, breathing through three carbs and twin pipes, is not a sound one soon forgets. You're sailing along on a warm autumn day, top down, the wind in your hair.

You're wide open, exposed to all the world, grinning from ear to ear. Still, it is the *sound*, like an old speedboat from the '50s. It just grabs you. The car is a '54 Corvette and though the year is 1991, you might as well turn back the clock 37 years or so.

There is a reason why people like Harley Earl, General Motors' styling chief in 1952, wanted the giant corporation to build a two-place open roadster like this Corvette. Though some would argue that there is no reason for a car to have only two seats (forget the fact that it has no side windows or outside door handles), there is no room for logic in an equation like this. You have to let your spirit take over. Letting go is what this car is all about.

Today, people stop dead in their tracks when they see a vintage Corvette pass them by. Much in the same way that the Vette bowled them over at GM's Motorama Show at the Waldorf-Astoria in New York City in 1953.

At the time, Chevrolet was suffering greatly from an image problem—basically, it didn't have one. Ford owned the youth market; other cars were more luxurious or faster. Chevrolet made dopey, staid, six-cylinder sedans. Say the word "Chevrolet" and you could hear a collective yawn across the American continent.

(Of course, this didn't stop these same staid Americans from buying Chevys. They did—by the millions. It was the world's largest-selling brand 18 years running. This, more than anything else, probably allowed it to continue building the Corvette from 1953 to 1955, despite the fact that it was considered to be a complete failure, in terms of sales.)

But the world was a changing place. Servicemen coming back from Europe in the years following World War II had seen wonderful sports cars in England, Germany and Italy. For many of them, a hulking Chevrolet sedan was not exactly the proper reward after risking your life in a foxhole.

Many men, looking for automotive excitement, returned home and built flathead Ford-powered hot rods. Others decided that an MG or Jaguar was just the ticket. Harley Earl saw this, and thought that perhaps Chevy could get in on the

The third 1953 Corvette ever built and the oldest known survivor is seen here in 1990, with some of its competition: the Jaguar XK-120 (left) and the '55 Thunderbird. Note the Chevrolet passenger car wheel covers, which were fitted to the first 25 or so '53 Vettes.

ground floor and snap up a piece of what he saw to be a burgeoning market.

With that in mind, he had Bob McLean style a body and put Maurice Olley in charge of the chassis. By May of '52, a full-size model was presented to Ed Cole, Chevrolet's engineering chief, and GM president Harlow Curtis.

Cole immediately took the car to heart and Curtis said that if public acceptance were great enough, production was a possibility. That accomplished, the next step was to prepare a vehicle for the Motorama show circuit. At the time, Motorama was a traveling show for the company that made stops around the country and Canada with show cars, production cars, etc. It was very much like the mega international automobile shows that are a staple today, except only one company (GM)

was represented. It is estimated that over four million people saw the Corvette in its original form and the response was overwhelmingly favorable. So much so that it left no doubt that Chevy had to forge ahead with production. It started in June of 1953 at Chevrolet's Flint, Mich., assembly plant.

The plan was to sell the car in limited numbers to VIPs through its top dealerships around the U.S. Unfortunately, reponse, so promising at the Motorama shows, somehow disappeared once actual production started. In many ways, it is easy to see why. First and foremost, it was very expensive by 1953 standards at $3,498. The heater ($91.40) and the signal-seeking AM radio ($145.15) were the only options (though all '53s had them). Ill-fitting plastic side curtains and a balky manual convertible top were the only protection the

The less-than-remarkable Stovebolt Six powered the early Corvettes.

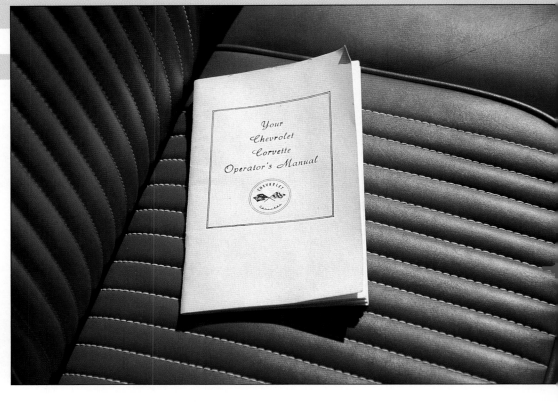

occupants had from the elements.

The first 25 or so cars built came with standard Chevrolet passenger car hubcaps and the first two didn't even have outside mirrors. All had the 235-cubic-inch "Blue Flame" Six, which was borrowed from the Chevrolet passenger car. Output was increased to 150 horsepower, thanks to a different camshaft and three Carter side-draft carbs, and it was hooked up to a two-speed Powerglide automatic transmission. A 3.55:1 axle ratio helped get you going. Wheelbase was 102.2 inches and width was 72.2 inches. It stood a mere 33 inches at the top of the door and the curb weight was 2,850 pounds, quite svelte for a car of that era. Acceleration was excellent by Chevrolet standards; however, it would get whipped by a new overhead valve V8 Oldsmobile or Buick.

No, there has never been any doubt that the first Corvette was not a proper sports car. Many saw it for what it was: basically, a late-'40s Chevy underneath with a beautiful fiberglass body and a hopped-up Stovebolt Six. What there was of a motoring press at the time scoffed at it. These journalists were mostly purists and they laughed at the Vette's handling, braking and, above all else, its automatic transmission.

Today, however, that doesn't seem to matter as much.

The body is the key. Undeniably beautiful, it was constructed of lightweight fiberglass—a first on a car—and every Corvette ever built has been made from this material. While we take this for granted today, when Saturns, Luminas and others are constructed at least in part from alternative materials, this abandonment of cold, hard steel was nothing short of revolutionary in 1953. It would be the Vette's first step toward becoming a technological leader.

As the 1953 model year closed out, only 183 of the 300 Corvettes built were sold. (All were Polo White with Sportsman Red interiors.) The rest were collecting dust on dealer lots and showroom floors, or being used for promotions. It didn't seem to matter, though. The people from the Bowtie division were positively cranked up over what they had done. It was reflected in their advertising and brochures.

In typical '50s hyperbole, Chevrolet called it the "American Sports Car of the Future" and bragged about its "amazing

The '54 Corvette was a virtual carryover. The biggest difference was the switch to a beige convertible top instead of black.

acceleration" and "very low center of gravity," not to mention its "jet-type tail, stop and direction signal lights." It bragged of its "strong plastic body," its "spacious, comfortable cockpit" and its "nearly vertical 17^1/4-inch-diameter steering wheel." Remember the "airplane-type instruments," which included the "hooded speedometer and radio speaker," and the "Transmission Selector Lever, floor-mounted in the sports car tradition."

For 1954, production was switched from Flint to St. Louis (where it would remain until the middle of the 1981 model year). Production increased for '54, up to 3,640 units, and the price decreased to $2,774. Three exterior colors—Pennant Blue, Sportsman Red and Black—were added, and all came with beige tops. Red, white and black cars came with red interiors; blue cars came with beige insides.

Midway though the model year, horsepower was nudged up to 155 by a redesign of the camshaft. Still no sign, however, of a manual transmission. The radios now carried the KC Conelrad national defense markings on the tuning face at 640 and 1240.

Chevrolet overproduced the '54 Corvette and had its hands full of them by year's end—to the tune of 1,076 cars. Things didn't look good for the Vette at this point. In fact, the sluggish sales helped kill a fastback model. Known as the Corvair, it made its debut at the '54 Motorama. Though well received, Chevrolet was already having second thoughts about Harley Earl's baby.

Sales literature pushed not only the sports car angle, but the luxury side as well. Of course, today we realize this car was hardly posh. But that is what sold automobiles then. Desperate times call for desperate actions.

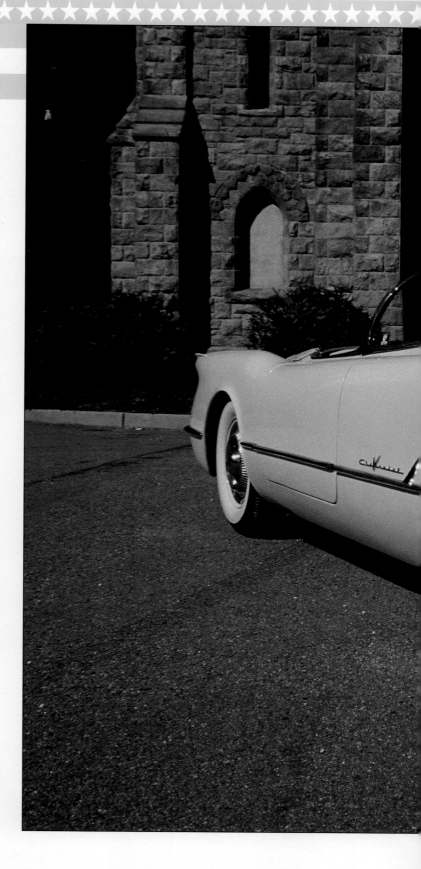

Domestic competition

Thank goodness for the 1955 Ford Thunderbird. If not for this car, the Corvette surely would never have seen 1956. The early Vette was unloved. With the introduction of the two-place Thunderbird, the Corvette had competition. Why bail out of the market when you already have an entry in place?

The key, then, was to make the Corvette a worthwhile challenger. Ford's T-Bird had a body that was not only made of steel, but manufactured by the Budd Company, which built train cars. This should give you an idea of how much more structurally sound it was over the plastic Corvette. With roll-up windows and an available hardtop, the Thunderbird had a definite advantage over the Vette from a practicality angle.

But good things were happening for the Corvette at Chevrolet. Ed Cole's V8 engine was introduced. Displacing 265 cubic inches and cranking out 195 horsepower, it replaced the plebian Blue Flame early in the model year. (Only a half-dozen six-cylinder Vettes were produced in '55.) Though hooked up to the same old Powerglide automatic, the V8 gave the Vette new-found vitality. It was definitely a match for the Thunderbird in the acceleration department.

For the record, it should be noted that there were some three-speed manual transmission-equipped '55 Corvettes. Just how many, though, remains a mystery to this day. A shift-for-yourself gearbox was never mentioned in sales literature; the best efforts by Corvette detectives have determined that 75 were so equipped. Unfortunately, it is very difficult to say

Gold "V" in the Chevrolet script identifies the '55 Corvette with bent-eight power, seen here in Gypsy Red.

for sure. Out of 700 '55s built, it is thought that fewer than 300 have survived—probably the highest attrition rate for any Vette model year.

If Chevrolet was excited about the '53 Corvette, it pulled out all the stops for the bent-eight version. "A cyclone of power with the new 195-h.p. V8 engine," the ads read. "A breath-stopping surge of power that surpasses anything you have ever imagined..." Hype or no, they weren't lying when they bragged of the 265 being "a dream powerplant ... ultra-compact, free-breathing, super-efficient." No, sir. So fantastic was the small-block V8 that it continues to power the Corvette to unprecedented levels of performance to this very day. If it is not the finest engine ever designed, it must be pretty close.

Aside from the obvious power difference, the eight-cylinder Vette welcomed a 12-volt electrical system. Those few cars powered by the straight Six were saddled with the 6-volt system. The V8s were identified from the outside by a large, gold V in the Chevrolet script on the front fender.

Corvette colors for '55 are a bit mysterious. Back again were Polo White and Pennant Blue; Gypsy Red replaced Sportsman Red, and two other hues, Corvette Copper and Harvest Gold, were added. It is possible, however, that some cars were built in Silver Grey.

The 1955 model would be the last year that the Corvette would be an honest-to-goodness roadster (an open two-seater with no outside door handles or side windows). Only an absolute purist, however, would lament its passing. The next generation, introduced in 1956, was a quantum leap forward and would build a reputation that will help carry the Vette into the 21st century.

Unwanted and unloved when new, early Corvettes never fail to attract a crowd today.

17

Chapter Two
The Coming of Duntov and the Age of Fuel Injection

Few people are as closely associated with a single automobile as Zora Arkus-Duntov is with the Corvette. Henry Ford and Enzo Ferrari come to mind, but they owned their own companies. Duntov, a Belgian-born, German- and Russian-educated engineer, was merely a Chevrolet employee.

Yet, he has become so entwined with Corvette history and legend that enthusiasts almost never speak of the cars without mentioning his name.

That Duntov retired as the Corvette's chief engineer at the end of 1974 doesn't seem to matter very much. He traverses the country year-round, attending Corvette shows, vintage races—anything automotive related. When the ribbon was cut for the opening of the National Corvette Museum in Bowling Green, Ky., he was the man holding the scissors. Born Christmas Day, 1909, he maintains as rigorous a schedule as men only half his age.

That he is known today as the "Father of the Corvette" is really quite humorous. He didn't even work for Chevrolet when the sports car's plans were being developed. He arrived on the scene soon after its introduction, and marveled at what he called, "a sheep in wolf's clothing." Soon he would be working on the V8 engine project and altering the course of the model's history forever.

When the 1956 Corvette arrived, it was a completely different automobile. The body, while maintaining some of the earlier car's styling themes (a toothy chrome grille, single round taillights and a wraparound windshield for starters), was totally revamped. The nose, raked back on the early cars, was now almost completely vertical. The side coves, today an early Vette trademark, appeared for the first time. Even 35 years after the fact, few cars are more beautiful.

But when it came to the long-term survival of the car, probably nothing was more important that the arrival of outside door handles, roll-up side windows and a manageable folding soft top. An optional hardtop was icing on the cake. Finally, the Corvette was becoming a real car.

Despite the fact that the chassis hadn't changed from the previous generation, Duntov reworked the suspension to make it a decent handler. He used wedges in front to increase caster and he relocated the rear spring hangers. The rear axle was new as well, and sported the same standard 3.55:1 ratio as its predecessor. Now, though, a 3.27 cog was optional with either the Powerglide or the new three-speed synchromesh transmission.

More big news was under the hood. The base engine received a 15-horsepower increase, thanks to a compression ratio that was upped from 8:1 to 9.25:1. Better still, the first optional V8 engines became available. The first sported a pair of Carter four-barrel carburetors on a cast aluminum intake manifold and put out 225 horsepower at 5200 rpm.

The new-for-'56 Corvette featured roll-up windows, outside door handles and a manageable soft top. Styling is timeless, as beautiful today as it was then.

The second added what has become known as the "Duntov" cam to the first package and made an astounding 240 horsepower at 5800 rpm. And this from only 265 cubic inches.

Finally, both performance *and* luxury could be touted. It was called "a true-blooded, tiger-tempered sports car in the noblest tradition. Whip-lash acceleration, cat-sure cornering and handling are matched with positive safety braking and the vivid luxury of its saddle-stitched bucket seats ..."

Better yet, "Let it rain, let it snow! Corvette offers the convenience of roll up regulators that quickly raise and lower the new windows ..."

The accent was on performance, but convenience akin to the Thunderbird's was a major selling point. The public responded with their wallets. Production increased to 3,467 units and would continue to go up annually until 1967. It is interesting to note that the Thunderbird, while still trouncing the Vette in the sales wars, was already leaning more toward the personal luxury market, now festooned with Continental spare tire kits, porthole-equipped hardtops, etc. After 1957, it would grow to a four-seater and leave the Corvette alone in its class again.

But Ford knew when to get out. So much good was happening in the Corvette camp in 1957 that even a supercharger on the Thunderbird's 312 V8 went almost completely unnoticed. For starters, '57 was the year that Rochester Ramjet fuel injection appeared on the Vette. Largely the

result of the work of Duntov and Harry Barr, motors so equipped would run the dynos up to 290 horsepower. This from a V8 now displacing 283 cubic inches. For advertising purposes, the new "fuelie" engines would put out 283 horsepower, or "one horsepower per cubic inch," long a magical figure in the world of high performance.

The ads said it all: "Fantastico. Even in Turin no one has fuel injection." And "Chevy exposed the biggest auto news of 1957—FUEL INJECTION." With the addition of a fully synchronized four-speed Borg-Warner gearbox, the Corvette was now a "proper" sports car. It apologized to no one. You simply couldn't buy a faster American car.

To be completely accurate, there were two basic versions of the fuelie, which appeared midway through the model year: a 250-horse version and two of the 283-horse variety. The lower-performance fuel injection engine had a milder hydraulic-lift camshaft, the high output jobs a new solid-lifter bumpstick. If you ordered RPO 579B, you got a "street" version, a beast that could click off 14-second quarter-mile times or, with the right gears, see the far side of 140 mph.

Check off RPO 579E, however, and you got a whole lot more. Available only with the heavy-duty brake and racing suspension package (RPO 684; $725), you got what is now known as an air-box Vette. For $675 extra, you got "elephant ear" air ducts to cool the front brakes, a fiberglass box on the inside left front fender to send air to the fuel injection unit and the left rear brake, and a corrugated hose on the right side

Air-box Corvettes (RPO 579E) were basically factory-ordered race cars. "Elephant ears" (right) ducted air to the front brakes, while a box inside the left front fender sent air to the fuel injection unit and the left rear brake. A hose on the right side ducted air to the right rear brake (middle, far right).

of the engine compartment to channel air from the nose to the right rear brake.

Though the brakes would continue to be a weak link in the Corvette until the introduction of all-wheel discs in 1965, nothing else about the Vette could be faulted. Do you want a boulevard tourer? Then, get power windows and top, stick with the base 220-hp engine and automatic tranny. Feel like a little fun? Order either the 245-horse or 270-horse dual quad motors with the four-speed. Wanna be king of the mountain? Fuel injection is the only way to fly. Also new for '57 were optional performance axle ratios, with 3.70, 4.11 and 4.56:1 available. Now you could better fine tune the engine to the drivetrain to suit your needs

As a performer, the Corvette was now the American flagship—no ifs, ands or buts. Its day as a true technological leader, from top to bottom, were still a few years off in the future.

What's it like to ride in a fuelie Corvette? It's almost otherwordly. First, especially in a '50s fuelie, you don't sit in the bucket seats. You sit *on* them, for they are bucket seats in name only. The sound is deliciously mechanical and loud. The solid lifters clatter away under the aluminum valve

---

Redesigned interior of the '58 has tach mounted on the steering column, in front of the driver. The radio and heater controls moved to the central console, where they remain to this day.

covers, the air rushes into the fuel injection unit. Out back is the unmistakable rumble of the small-block Chevy at idle. Rev it up, dump the clutch and you are in adrenaline city. The skinny old bias-ply tires are so absolutely overmatched, it's a joke. This is what burning rubber is all about. First, second, third, fourth—it doesn't matter. You're getting scratch in all of 'em. The world is passing you by at an astounding rate and you just want more.

It's pure bliss. You're watching the driver wrestle with the gigantic round steering wheel, the speedometer is sailing into never-never land and the tach is headed for the red zone. The world is a much better place from behind a wraparound windshield.

For 1958, Corvette styling kept right up with the times. Which means it got bigger, wider and more garish than ever before. It sprouted quad headlights, was nine inches longer and more than two inches wider. Two chrome strips extended down the center of the front fenders, from the headlights back. For good measure, there were two chrome bands running down the decklid as well.

As you might expect, weight was up. Some 200 pounds were added, pushing the Vette past the 3,000-pound mark for the first time ever. Price rose some $400, making the base Corvette a $3,591 item. It didn't seem to matter, though. Production was up close to 30 percent, with 9,168 automobiles coming out of the St. Louis plant.

The interior was redesigned to feature the tach above the steering column, with the heater controls and radio mounted in a central console. The passenger side of the dash featured a handy grab handle.

The '58 Corvette in Signet Red.

Under the new washboard-style hood, things were pretty much a carryover from the year before. The standard mill was now rated at 230 horsepower (up 10 from '57), but the optional carbureted motors remained at 245 and 270 horses respectively. For the new year, Chevy decided to rate the top fuelie at its actual power output, 290 ponies, while the lower-performance fuel injection engine stayed at 250.

Exterior color choices went down from seven to six, with the hues changing from vibrant colors to more pastels. Signet Red, almost a rose color, replaced Venetian Red. Charcoal

was added to the list, as was Panama Yellow, another soft color. Black disappeared until 1959, with Regal Turquoise, Silver Blue and Snowcrest White the only other choices. All could be had, of course, with contrasting side coves, thus increasing your color choices.

If 1958 was a year of great change, then 1959 was basically a carryover. Happily, two of the garish styling tricks of the previous model disappeared. Say goodbye to the washboard hood, which became smooth, and adios to the chrome strips on the rear decklid. Overall, the appearance was much cleaner. Colors returned to the more vibrant variety, with Roman Red, Tuxedo Black and Inca Silver topping the list.

Perhaps because '58 was such a turbulent (as well as successful) year, there seemed little need to alter much on the Corvette. A T-handle reverse lockout shifter became standard on the manual transmission, black became an interior color choice for the first time and a storage bin was added under the passenger-side grab bar. For the first time, you could order your Vette with sun visors. Not exactly earth-shattering stuff.

The real story for 1959 had nothing to do with the production Corvette. No, the most important '59 Vette of all was one you couldn't buy.

It was called the Sting Ray racer.

Styling on the '59 Corvette was cleaned up considerably. Much of the excess chrome was removed, leaving just a gorgeous design.

Born out of the credo that racing improves the breed, the Sting Ray was the result of three years of efforts by Duntov and his engineers to make the Corvette a viable race car. Their earlier efforts—the SS (which hit 183 mph on GM's Phoenix Proving Ground in December 1958), the SR-2 and the SS Mule chassis—were all part of the evolution of the Sting Ray.

After a lot of hard work came the Automobile Manufacturers Association's ban on auto racing and, suddenly, such endeavors were in jeopardy. The mule chassis had under-

The magnificent Sting Ray racer at speed with Dr. Dick Thompson behind the wheel, seen here in 1989 on the vintage racing circuit.

gone extensive development and was going to be used for Chevrolet's all-out assault on LeMans. Tested by such luminaries as Stirling Moss and Juan Manuel Fangio, it sat for a year while Bill Mitchell tried to figure out what to do with it. Finally, he purchased it himself and had budding automotive designer and GM newcomer Larry Shinoda adapt a sleek new body to it. Christened the Sting Ray, it was Mitchell's personal property. He and Duntov were going racing.

Originally painted red (it would later be silver, the color it remains to this day), the Sting Ray made its debut on April 18, 1959, at the President's Cup at Marlboro Raceway. Despite limited track testing, the lack of a limited-slip differential and a brake system that would prove itself inadequate, it finished fourth in its maiden outing.

Power, naturally, came from a fuel-injected small-block displacing 283 cubic inches. It was rated at 280 horsepower at 6200 rpm and would rev to 6800. Helping breathing was an experimental set of aluminum cylinder heads. It was plenty fast, with a curb weight of some 2,000 pounds, but aerody-

namics and brakes would hinder it throughout the season. But like the production Corvette, its best days were still ahead of it. In 1960, it would go on to win the SCCA C-production title, finishing miles ahead in the points standings.

The 1960 production cars, though outwardly similar to the '59s, were much improved machines. An anti-roll bar in the rear helped engineers eliminate the heavy-duty rear springs. Up front, a larger-diameter roll bar was added. Cast aluminum cylinder heads were to be introduced, but were found lacking in durability. It is questionable whether any ever made it onto a production engine.

Inside the small-block, the compression ratio was bumped

For 1961, the production Vette got a new tail,
first seen on the Sting Ray racer in 1959. It had four
round taillamps, a Corvette trademark for 30 model years.

up a half point, to 11:1. Horsepower increased to 315 in the top fuelie motor, and to 275 in the lower-horse fuelie. Ratings on the carbureted engines stayed the same. Those equipped with the Duntov cam got a new aluminum radiator as an added bonus. Not only was it lighter, but it provided better cooling as well.

Other interesting options were a 24-gallon gas tank, which took up so much room in the convertible top storage well that it necessitated the deletion of the soft roof. These Corvettes became hardtop-only vehicles. Metallic brakes, first introduced in '59, were back again.

Prices now started at $3,872 and for the first time, more than 10,000 people—10,261 to be precise—thought that was a good deal and plunked their money down for a Corvette.

The year 1961 will be remembered for the start of one Corvette tradition and the end of some others. It was the first year for the use of four round taillights, a style that lasted until 1991 when they were replaced by four ZR-1-type rectangular units. (Chevy stylists are quick to defend their actions by stating the taillights are "oval-shaped," not square.)

The teeth in the grille, reduced in number from 13 to nine in 1958, would disappear altogether in '61 as the Vette received a major facelift. The entire car from the doors back resembled the Sting Ray racer and gave fans a glimpse of what the 1963 production Corvette Sting Ray would be. Gone was the large, round nose emblem. Instead, the word "Corvette" would be spelled out up front. The contrasting

RPO Corvettes got a heavy-duty suspension and brakes, along with fuel injection, and are identifiable by their "dog dish" hubcaps. This one is a '62.

The '63 split-window Corvette blew away the automotive world when it debuted in the fall of '62. Like many '63s, this particular car wears aluminum knock-off wheels, though they weren't available on production vehicles until 1964.

color in the side cove would become a part of history after the '61 model year ended.

It would also mark the last year for the venerable 283 V8, which would grow to 327 cubic inches in '62. Sadly, it also marked the end of multiple-carbureted small-blocks.

Despite the fact that the powerplants were essentially carryovers, you'd still have been hard-pressed to find a more potent automobile on the road. But the era of the musclecar was rapidly approaching. The Corvette was in for some stiff competition.

For '62, Chevrolet bored and stroked the small-block to bring it up to 327 cubic inches. Funny thing about engines. Some combinations of bore and stroke work better than others. For Ed Cole's V8, this may have been the perfect size. Horsepower, even in the base car, jumped to 250. First up on the option ladder was the 300-horse 327, which sported a single Carter AFB four-barrel. Next on the agenda was the 340-horse solid-lifter job, also with a Carter AFB. If you found fuel injection to your taste, you got a fire-breathing 360 horses.

The base price of a Corvette exceeded $4,000 for the first time, with the cheapest model coming in at $4,038. (It is interesting to note that in 1960, the base price of the Vette went down $3, despite the addition of more standard features. That kind of thing just doesn't happen anymore.)

Not to trivialize the '62 Corvette, but what came next was

an automobile that would set the world on its ear. Everyone who waited for the Corvette to become a true world-class sports car, a technological innovator, was stunned by the 1963 Corvette Sting Ray.

In one fell swoop, Chevrolet introduced a car so insanely beautiful, so powerful, so right, that even the manufacturers of the imported sports cars were forced to take notice. Available for the first time in either coupe or convertible form, the Sting Ray was a world-beater. Features included hideaway headlamps, incredibly rare in '63, a split rear window on the coupe, a completely new (and proper) interior, which had adjustable seats, and an adjustable steering column standard. Best of all was the crowning jewel, hidden beneath the car where no one could see it: the independent rear suspension.

No, the Vette was not the first American car to have IRS. But the Vette's system actually worked. Handling was not to be believed. The IRS would soak up the bumps like it was nobody's business and kept the car stable in turns. The front

suspension, while still of the coil spring variety, was much improved. Gone were the god-awful kingpins, which dated back to the '40s. Now there was a ball-joint-equipped front end. Steering was all-new and, for the first time, a power assist was available.

Think about this: As we head for the 21st century, few other V8-powered American cars have IRS. And only the Corvette could be considered a performance car.

Styling was so close to the '59 Sting Ray racer that it left onlookers breathless. Few people could find anything wrong with it, though Duntov and Mitchell argued endlessly about the bar that divided the rear window. After driving a production model, Mitchell finally relented, agreeing that it hindered vision, and it was eliminated in 1964.

There was no longer any doubt. The Corvette Sting Ray

was the flagship of the American auto industry.

Chevrolet was not about to stand pat. With St. Louis working double shifts and 21,513 units sold, it continued to improve the breed for '64. The six-inch-wide aluminum knock-off wheels, originally scheduled to debut the previous year, finally appeared as an option. Quality problems (porosity) prohibited their being factory-installed on the '63, although by the end of the model run they were available as an over-the-counter item. Thanks to a new solid-lifter cam, power was up again, to 365 ponies from the carbureted 327 and to 375 from the fuelie, which through constant development was working better than ever.

Better still to harness this newfound power was a new four-speed transmission from GM's Muncie division (which first appeared late in the 1963 model year). The M-20 could be had with both wide and close ratios for $188.30. Slick-shifting, accurate and bulletproof, this gearbox was a real boost to the Sting Ray—it didn't matter if you were on the road, a drag strip or a twisty race course.

The chassis was upgraded for better handling and ride and less vibration and noise. New springs (front and rear), better shocks and rubber body mounts were among the improvements.

When the 1965 Corvette appeared, it was again a more refined, more powerful and safer vehicle—thanks to the introduction (finally) of four-wheel-disc brakes. Regrettably, it was the last year for the fuel-injected small-block. Though it could be tuned easily by a competent mechanic (and its performance potential was never questioned), advances in carb technology as well as the introduction of the more powerful and cheaper Mark IV big-block sealed its fate. At $538, the Mega-Mouse was an expensive commodity. In an era when cubic inches were everything, more people were interested in the 396, which put out 50 additional horsepower and cost $245.30 less. A mere 771 customers shelled out for the fuelie before it disappeared late in the model year.

But there is more to the story of the '65 Corvette than just the end of the age of fuel injection.

The last of the fuelies: the '65 Corvette Sting Ray. Say goodbye to Ramjet fuel injection, which helped make the Vette a legend the world over.

Chapter Three

Cubes Are King

There was never a more exciting time for car lovers than the musclecar era of the 1960s and early '70s. Detroit was engaged in an all-out, win-at-any-cost horsepower struggle. Never before or since has there been anything like it. The Big Three waged war on the street, on the race tracks and in car magazines.

No longer would high-strung smaller engines make the grade. Cubic inches were everything. While Chrysler was finding a great deal of success with its 413 and 426 Max Wedge monsters and Ford's 427 would soon dominate NASCAR, Chevrolet was stuck with its 409.

And even if the 409 was "real fine," Zora Arkus-Duntov and the rest of Chevy's engineering team knew that its full potential had already been reached. With that in mind, they went back to the drawing board and came up with the modified-wedge head Mark IV big-block. With a bore of 4.094 and a stroke of 3.76 inches, it displaced 396 cubic inches and had an 11.0:1 compression ratio. (According to Duntov, the engineers were originally planning to go for 427 cubes, but hesitated because they believed NASCAR was going to impose a 400-inch limit. When they saw that wouldn't be the case, the engine was enlarged for the following year.)

The block was cast of high-chromium iron and featured four-bolt main bearings. The crank was a steel forging, swinging heavy-duty connecting rods and TRW forged aluminum pistons. The camshaft was, naturally, of the high-lift, solid-lifter variety, and the engine was fed by an 800-cfm Holley carb on a high-rise intake manifold.

Where the Rat motor differed from all previous Chevy engines, however, was in its use of a "semi-hemi" valvetrain layout. The intake and exhaust valves were arranged at odd angles, thus allowing the use of larger valves for better breathing. The ports were individually spaced and the valves positioned to produce optimum flow characteristics. The inlet valves were actually tipped toward the inlet port to minimize the amount of direction change the incoming mixture must take. The exhaust valves, on the other hand, were tipped away from the inlet valve and toward its extra-large radius port.

The incredible breathing capabilities of these heads

The 396 big-block engine appeared midway through the 1965 model year. With 425 horsepower, it was the most powerful Corvette yet. All-wheel disc brakes, standard for '65, gave the Sting Ray stopping power equal to its acceleration capabilities.

helped the Corvette's 396 pump out 425 horsepower. Not only was this more than one horsepower per cubic inch (a figure thought to be almost unobtainable less than 10 years before), but it came from an engine that was substantially larger than had ever been installed in a Vette by the factory.

With all this newfound power and torque (460 lbs.-ft.), it should come as no surprise that the Corvette needed some strengthening in the drivetrain area. First, the standard transmission would be the close-ratio M-21 four-speed. (The Saginaw three-speed standard with the base small-block would probably last about an hour behind the 396.) Chevy engineers also strengthened the rear wheel spindle arm and the bracket support assembly, and the rear driveshaft univer-

sal joints were converted to heavy-duty capscrew models. A rear stabilizer bar was added and the one up front was increased in diameter. The standard rear screw with the big-block was the 3.08 with Positraction. Ratios as low as 4.56:1 were available, but only a serious drag racer would opt for that cog.

From a technological standpoint, the biggest news for '65 was not the introduction of the big-block, which occurred in April. The real news, which would have a much greater impact over the long haul, was that four-wheel disc brakes finally became standard equipment on the Vette. Developed by Delco, the Corvette (at last) had a brake system that was up to the performance of the car—not that the earlier brakes

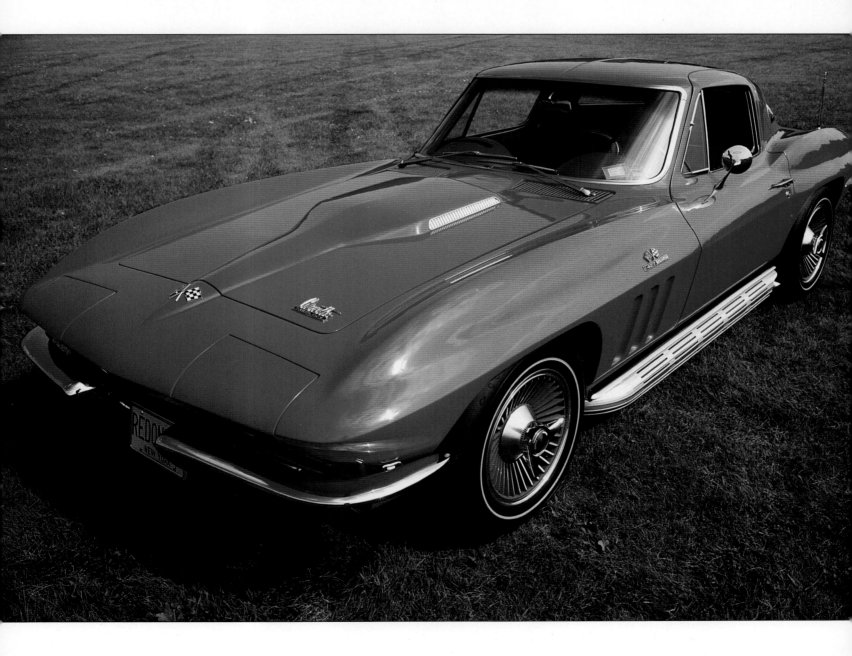

were dangerous, but racing proved time and again that the drums were inadequate for serious high-performance use.

For a bit of perspective, go to some car dealers today and see how many vehicles can be purchased with four-wheel discs, even as an extra-cost option. The number is alarmingly low. Yet, they've been standard on the Vette for more than 25 years.

As if the '65 Corvette wasn't fast enough, Duntov and his band of merry men took the fiberglass wundercar a step further for '66. That meant increasing the 396 to 427 cubic inches. All it took was an increase in the bore to 4.25 inches.

Presto! Combined with the high-lift, long-duration solid-lift camshaft, the 396's big brother was rated at an astonishing 450 horsepower at 5600 rpm. Glory days, indeed.

Concerned over how the public (read: insurance companies and the burgeoning safety lobby) would react to such a high number, Chevrolet later lowered the rating to "only" 425 horsepower. In a November 1965 road test, *Car and Driver* said it would take Chevrolet's word for it, but "we feel compelled to point out that these are 425 horses of the size and strength never before seen by man ..."

Its test car, with optional 3.36:1 gears, ran the quarter-mile

The Rat motor grew to 427 cubic inches in '66. Originally, the two versions were rated at 400 and 450 hp; later cars were tagged at a more conservative 390 and 425 hp, respectively.

The '67 was the most refined Sting Ray to date. This one has the ultra-desirable 435-horse 427 with Tri-Power.

in 12.8 seconds at 112 mph—on standard street rubber, no less. Opting for a 3.70, 4.11 or 4.56 screw would send you into the mid-12s.

Also new for '66 was a more mild-mannered 427, one with a special hydraulic-lifter cam and lower compression ratio. This was rated at 400 horsepower initially, but in 99 percent of the cars delivered with this engine, it was rated at "only" 390 horsepower. With a decent driver, it was good for mid- to high-13-second ETs. Think about it: The second most powerful Corvette engine was at least as fast as a Chrysler Hemi-powered anything. And it could stop and handle. The only thing on the street that could touch a big-block Vette was a 427 Cobra and you didn't see them very often.

Chevrolet disappointed the automotive world in the fall of 1966. Everyone was expecting a radical new Corvette, in-spired by the Mako Shark II show car. Developmental problems put that machine off for a year; instead, the public got the most refined Sting Ray yet. A host of subtle styling tweaks and interior changes made for the best grand touring Vette yet.

If some were let down because there wasn't a new body, they could at least be content with the choice of powerplants available. The 327s were all carryovers from '66, coming in 300 and 350-horse form. Over in the big-block camp, incredibly exciting things were happening.

On the induction side, Chevrolet introduced a six-barrel system for its 427s. A trio of 350-cfm Holley two-barrels sat under a triangular air filter, providing 400 horsepower with the hydraulic lifter engine and 435 ponies with the solid lifter cam. The motor ran off the center carb and a vacuum linkage

New-for-'68 Vette was the wildest yet. With L-88 power (right), you had a store-bought race car.

Stingray name returned on the 1969 Corvette, now as one word.
Front fender louver trim was a '69-only option and cost $21.10.

system told the end carbs when to come on.

The new setup was at once a blessing and a curse. While it proved to be as smooth as fuel injection when running properly, it usually wasn't. Stumbling, hesitation, tuning headaches—you name it. The idea behind multiple carburetion was to make the big engine more pleasant to drive on the street. In tune, it did. And it did flow a delightfully grotesque 1050 cfm. But mechanical linkage is almost always more reliable than vacuum in such applications. By eschewing mechanical linkage, Chevrolet did its part to sell a lot of aftermarket intake manifolds and four-barrel carbs.

That Tri-Power cars are the most sought-after Corvettes today is a rather unusual irony.

Another significant option for the 435-horse Rat motor was RPO L-89, aluminum cylinder heads. Because of their high price ($368.65—almost the same as the L-71 engine option) and the fact that a motor so equipped did not receive a higher horsepower rating, only 16 people ordered them. Most were just not interested in the 75-pound weight savings and it wasn't until years later that people found out they actually added about 20 horses. They would remain on the option list for just three years, finding 624 takers in '68 and 390 in '69.

Historically, the most important news for '67 was the introduction of the L-88 powerplant. It was nothing short of a racing engine and Chevrolet did not market it as anything but. It had a 12.5:1 compression ratio, an aluminum intake manifold and heads, and a single 850-cfm Holley four-barrel sealed to the cowl-induction hood. A special high-lift solid-lifter cam, special valve springs, valve spring caps and oil seals were also part of the package, as was a heavy-duty clutch, smaller flywheel and a heavy-duty aluminum cross-flow radiator.

Not only were the cylinder heads aluminum, but they had cleaned-up intake and exhaust passages and ports and larger

1.84-inch exhaust valves (1.72 was standard).

And by opting for RPO L-88, you had to take RPO J-56 (heavy-duty power-assisted brakes with semi-metallic linings); F-41 (heavy-duty front and rear suspension); K-66 (full transistor ignition); and M-22 (heavy-duty, close-ratio four-speed transmission). What you *couldn't* get was a radio or a heater/defroster. Plus, the engine came with no pollution controls at all. It was strictly a race-only item, requiring 103 octane fuel. Only 20 hardy souls plunked down their cash for it in '67, but those who did got a race car that could run 11-second ETs right out of the box.

The L-88 option, while rated at five horsepower less than the L-71, actually pegged the dyno needle at 560 horses at 6400 rpm. In 1968, production would increase to 80 units, and then peak at 116 in 1969, its final year.

When the 1968 Corvette appeared, it was the wildest-looking automobile ever. Inspired by a mako shark that head stylist Bill Mitchell caught while fishing in Bimini, the new Vette actually looked like one of these killers of the deep, right down to the gills cut into the front fenders. (These gills aided aerodynamics by keeping air from building up under the car.) Its long, pointed nose was so low that the driver couldn't see it. The high arching front and rear fenders became a Corvette trademark. So inspired was the design, in fact, that GM would continue using it until 1982. And it sold extremely well until the last coupe rolled off the assembly line.

These are the only two factory ZL-1 Corvettes known to exist. Roger Judski of Maitland, Fla., recently bought the yellow car for $300,000 from federal marshals. White car is in the collection of former <u>Los Angeles Times</u> publisher Otis Chandler.

The LT-1 was the last solid lifter-equipped small-block Chevy built, and possibly the most powerful. It produced 370 hp in the Corvette. This '70 features non-stock aluminum wheels, which became available in 1976.

While the look of the '68 was completely different, the engines and chassis were essentially the same. The battery was moved from under the hood to a compartment behind the driver's seat for better weight distribution and handling. Wheel width increased from six to seven inches to help handling (it would go up again, to eight inches, in 1969). A larger front anti-roll bar was used on the big-blocks, up to 0.875 inch from 0.750. Rat-motored Vettes also got a 0.562-inch bar out back. On all Corvettes, the spring rates were stiffer than they were the previous year and the power steering was of the higher effort variety. The resulting package was a much faster car on a road course that tended to understeer more than its predecessor.

Aside from the far-out styling, what really set the car apart from the pack were the removable roof panels and rear window on the coupe. Chevrolet had originally wanted the '68 coupe to have a targa-style roof. It found, however, that without any support body flex was unacceptable. The solution, borrowed from Gordon M. Buehrig, was a steel brace that connected the windshield to the roof. The single removable panel would give way to two panels and—ta-da—the open coupe was born. (Most people erroneously call this design the T-top or T-roof. It was never referred to as such by Chevrolet.)

The rear window, released by two catches, came out and was stored inside the car in a tray under the rear deck lid. It

Though Chevrolet never sold LS-7-powered Corvettes, people sometimes built their own. This one uses an aluminum Can-Am block. Production versions were to have cast-iron blocks.

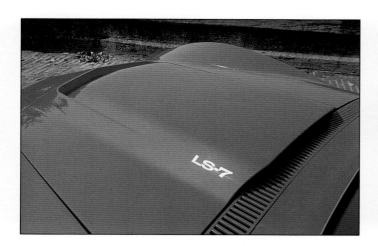

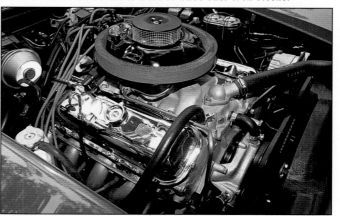

was a neat idea that helped cool what could be a very hot interior on non-air conditioned cars. Cost considerations rendered it history after the 1972 model year.

Another interesting interior feature that debuted in '68 was a fiber-optic monitoring system for the vehicle's exterior lights. A glance at the console could tell you if a bulb was burned out and, if so, precisely which one it was. That was neat, but it too became a victim of the bean counters, going away after the 1971 model year.

The 1969 Corvette will be remembered for many fine features, but more than anything else, it was the pinnacle of the performance years. No fewer than eight engines were available, including six versions of the 427. The 327 was enlarged to 350 cubes and could be had with either 300 (base) or 350 horsepower. A third 350, the 370-horse LT-1, was scheduled, but wouldn't join the party until 1970.

In the big-block camp, the 390, 400 and two versions of the 435-horsepower engine were available. So, too, was the L-88. But a new player, offered for no less a tariff than $3,000, was introduced.

The LS-6 finally appeared in the Corvette in '71. With 425 hp, it was the last great Rat motor.

Known as RPO ZL-1, it was an all-aluminum version of the much-heralded L-88. Horsepower was said to be in the 580 range, but the real kicker was its light weight.

Models tested by the press weighed less than 3,000 pounds and could accelerate to 1,320 feet in under 11 seconds. Top speed was, theoretically, in the 180-mph range with proper gearing. It was—and is—the most ferocious Corvette of all time.

And the rarest as well. It is believed that only two ZL-1 Stingrays were ever built, though certainly more were assembled by dealers and racers. Others believe that perhaps as many as 10 were built, but their whereabouts remain a mystery more than two decades later.

Things would never again be this wild. For 1970, the big-block grew to 454 cubic inches and made 390 horsepower. Unfortunately, the 450-horse LS-6, which became a legendary powerplant in the Chevelle SS, didn't find its way into the Vette's engine bay for 1970. Worse still, neither did the even more powerful (460-hp) LS-7. A 425-horse version of the LS-6 appeared in '71, but the more expensive LS-7, a larger displacement version of the fabled L-88, never made the game.

Don't shed too many tears, however. The solid-lifter-

A 1971 LT-1 coupe.

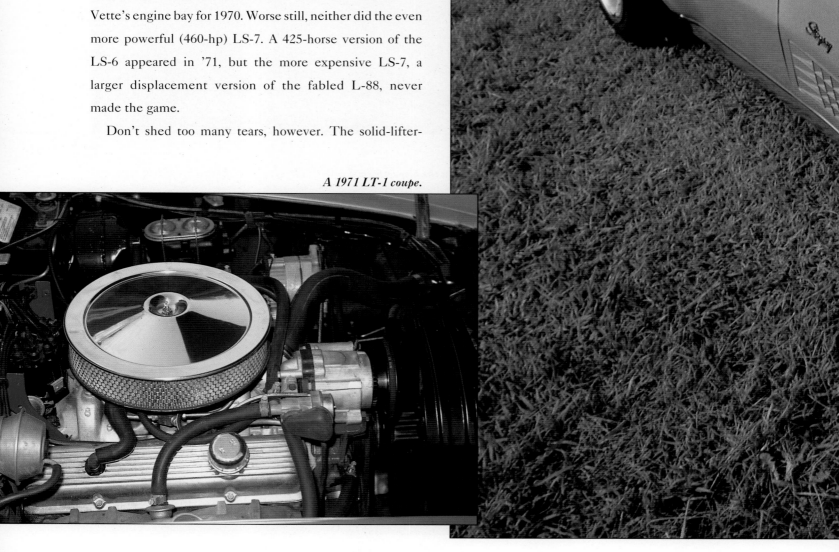

equipped LT-1 finally made it under the hood of the Corvette and it was, quite possibly, the most powerful small-block ever built. It delivered big-block performance, capable of sending the Vette to low-13-second elapsed times on street tires with closed exhausts.

The Vette benefited annually from increased comfort and refinement. It was truly an all-purpose GT car, capable of transporting two in comfort with the ability to run circles around other machines on the race track.

Sadly, with increasing pressure from the insurance companies and environmentalists, the power of the Corvette began declining in '71 and wouldn't level off for another 10 years. The Corvette, expected to become a mid-engined vehicle in the early '70s and an all-wheel-drive machine by the middle of the decade, suffered from severe neglect by General Motors. Its engineers were having enough troubles getting their engines to run, strangled as they were by pollution control devices.

The Corvette (as well as other high-performance American cars) was considered frivolous by the higher-ups. As long as it sold reasonably well, there was no reason to improve or

Owned by Jack Howell, this '72 could be the last pre-'90 ZR-1 ever built.

The '72 LT-1 was the only high-performance, solid-lifter engine Chevy ever offered with air conditioning. Only 18 convertibles were so equipped.

change it. The solid-lifter LT-1 was replaced by the less potent L-82 in '73 and the 454 wouldn't live to see 1975 in the Vette. Duntov, literally a legend in his own time, was forced out by mandatory retirement at age 65. Dave McLellan, a more conservative, management-oriented person, took Duntov's place as chief engineer.

Convertibles were discontinued after 1975, and it wouldn't be until March 1983 that the world would see the next-generation Corvette. The years in between would not be good ones. With Chevy pumping out almost 50,000 copies a year, quality control took a back seat. (Sales peaked at 53,807 in '79.) And while decent performance could still be obtained by checking off the correct boxes on the option sheet, most buyers didn't do so. The Corvette was becoming a very expensive, two-seat Monte Carlo—more a tool for middle-aged men trying to recapture their youth than a serious enthusiast's automobile.

Like many of its buyers, the Corvette got old and fat. By the late '70s, a Vette would tip the scales at close to 3,800 pounds. Unfortunately, this malaise was not restricted to the plastic Chevy. It was a reflection of the American auto industry in general. Even with technology that dated back to the mid-'50s (the engine) and early '60s (the chassis), the Vette was still the flagship of the fleet. But it had taken on a lot of water by 1982.

The L-82 (opposite) was the top small-block available in 1973.

The last big-block was the 1974 454 (above), while the final convertible was the '75 (below).

Chapter Four
The Current Generation:
Worth Waiting For

Depending on who you believe, work on the "next" generation Corvette started sometime around the late 1960s or early '70s. Using sound logic and current information, most believed that the new Vette introduced in 1968 would be the last front-engined model. A world-class, mid-engined supercar would appear to take its place sometime around 1972 or '73.

Indeed, Chevrolet teased the automotive world with a variety of mid-engined prototypes—some V8-powered, others of the rotary engine variety. Some were made of fiberglass, others aluminum. Zora Arkus-Duntov had plans ready, not only for a mid-engined rocket but for an all-wheel-drive version as well. It came *thisclose* to actually seeing production.

Unfortunately, the Corvette became a victim of its own success. Because it was selling better than ever before, GM decided not to mess with a proven money-maker.

When the Mako Shark's replacement actually arrived as a 1984 model, it was—and remains to this day—of the traditional front-engine, rear-drive layout. Is this reason to lament? Perhaps, given the virtues inherent in the mid-engine design. On the other hand, the newest Corvette has taken the front-engine, rear-drive design to unprecedented levels. It is almost an art form. When it was introduced, almost nothing handled like it—certainly nothing in its $25,000 price range. The same is essentially true today. Very few cars on the road can touch it.

Nor does the current design suffer any of the usual drawbacks inherent in the mid-engine design, such as over-complexity or a lack of storage space. The Vette is easier and less expensive to work on. A person only has to remember the Pontiac Fiero fiasco to appreciate the front-engine design. Someone once said, "You are in big trouble when you have to work on an American car through the trunk."

This is not to say that Chevrolet couldn't do a good job with a mid-engined model. Duntov still swears by his design and after seeing the blueprints it does seem almost flawless. Somehow, though, you get the feeling that in the late 20th century, GM is better off sticking with what it knows best.

By 1983, the Corvette had been on a weight reduction

Interior of the '84 Vette was all new. It featured excellent seats and ergonomics, but was criticized for its digital display instrument panel. The chassis for the new car (right) is a work of art, with exotic alloys everywhere.

The man behind the current Corvette, chief engineer Dave McLellan.

The all-new '84 retained the traditional Corvette styling themes. Gone were the old-fashioned removable roof panels; in their place was a simpler, one-piece targa roof that unbolted to let the sunshine in.

The '85 Corvette coupe.

program for a couple of years. Still, when the new model appeared at around 3200 pounds, some were disappointed. That was about all that upset anyone. With 205 base horsepower on tap, superior aerodynamics and long-legged gearing, 140 mph was attainable in an American car for the first time in a decade. So were low-15-second ETs at the drags; 60 mph would come up in less than seven seconds. While those numbers are reachable by several cars today, at that time only an Italian exotic or Porsche 928 could better the Vette. It was, by a wide margin, the fastest car made in America, and ranked with the fastest half-dozen cars in the world regardless of price or national origin.

The real story of the '84 Corvette (Chevrolet celebrated the 30th anniversary of its sports car by *not* building a 1983 model) was its

The Corvette convertible returned in 1986 after an 11-year absence. It was chosen to pace the Indy 500 that year, and all '86 roadsters were designated Pace Car Replicas.

The '86 roadster at speed.

chassis and suspension. Sure, the traditional transverse rear leaf spring that first appeared on the '63 Sting Ray returned, but now it was made of fiberglass reinforced plastic. Coil springs disappeared from the front end and were replaced with another transverse leaf spring, also made of lightweight but super-sturdy plastic.

The rear half shafts, rear differential support, front and rear suspension crossmembers, propeller shaft, torque converter and gearbox housing were all made from expensive aluminum alloy. So were the front A-arms, rear knuckles, and upper and lower control arms and struts. This was truly space-age stuff.

Steering was finally of the rack-and-pinion variety. The standard ratio was 15.5:1—plenty fast, but on the heavy-duty Z-51-equipped models a quicker 13.0:1 was standard.

These world-class suspension goodies would all be for naught without proper wheels and tires. Dave McLellan and his engineers knew this, and their solution was 16-inch-diameter wheels all around, with each designed to draw air to the brakes. Width was $8\frac{1}{2}$ inches, front and rear, on base-suspended cars; on Z-51 cars, it was $8\frac{1}{2}$ inches in front, $9\frac{1}{2}$ at the rear. (Some late base cars came with the Z-51 setup due to a shortage of $8\frac{1}{2}$-inch wheels.)

Goodyear and Chevrolet worked together to develop a tire specifically for the Corvette, an industry first. The result was

P255/50-VR16 "Gatorback" tires which, for the first time on a production car, were of the unidirectional design. Not only did these skins give the Corvette exceptional handling capabilities, but they enhanced braking as well. Plus, because they were developed from a Formula 1 rain tire, their behavior in the wet was unparalleled.

In the cockpit, things were also completely new. For better or worse, a colorful digital display instrument panel replaced the traditional analog gauges. A wider transmission tunnel allowed the car to be lowered, but intruded on interior space. The seats, both standard and the sport option, were the best ever installed in an American car, offering superior comfort and support for high-speed maneuvers.

Only the engine and four-speed automatic transmission were carried over from the '82 Corvette. Later in production, a new Doug Nash 4+3 manual transmission was offered as a no-cost option. It differed from a traditional gearbox in that overdrive ratios were available in second, third and fourth, controlled by the push of a button.

Chevrolet bragged in its ads that the new Vette was the

Option B2K—the Callaway Twin Turbo Corvette—debuted in 1987 and pumped out 345 horsepower.

The '88 Corvette with the new, standard 16-inch wheels. They were used for only one year.

most advanced production car on the planet and they weren't kidding. Better than that, it proved performance, fuel economy and clean exhaust emissions were not mutually exclusive. With the help of computers and brilliant engineers, it single-handedly ushered in the modern musclecar era.

Despite a base price of $21,800, sales hit 51,547 units in the extended model year. Buoyed by this success, Chevrolet kept the pressure on. A new "Tuned Port" fuel injection system

replaced Cross-Fire Injection, which was, in reality, nothing more than an electronic twin carb setup. Horsepower soared to 235 and quarter-mile times dipped into the mid-14-second range. Better still, top speed improved to over 150 mph. This was performance akin to an LS-6 big-block from 14 years earlier. Yet the new model delivered all this with air conditioning, stereo and power everything.

For '86, the convertible was reintroduced during the middle

Chevrolet offered an optional racing-inspired, dealer-installed body kit in 1988.

The Callaway Sledgehammer is the world's fastest street car, capable of 254.76 mph. It retains a full complement of luxury appointments such as air conditioning and stereo cassette.

The Paul Deutschman-designed Callaway Aerobody appeared in 1989. It's both beautiful and functional.

of the model year and it was chosen as the Pace Car for the Indianapolis 500. A total of 7,315 roadsters were built and not only were they all designated as "Pace Car" models, but they were equipped with aluminum cylinder heads as well.

Finally!

The Corvette was running with the best of the best, not only in America, but in Europe as well, thanks to a slightly more aggressive export program that began in 1984. But Chevrolet still had a couple of more aces up its corporate sleeve. Rumors had been running rampant about the possibility of a twin-turbocharged version for a couple of years and in 1987 it became a reality. Dubbed option B2K, the Callaway Corvette was born.

It was not inexpensive, that's for certain. But at $19,995 (in addition to the price of the car), you got a lot for your dough. The Vettes were assembled in Bowling Green and shipped to Callaway Cars in Old Lyme, Conn. There, Reeves Callaway's men would pore over each vehicle, installing a 345-horsepower 350 under the clamshell hood (into which a pair of NACA ducts

The 32-valve, LT-5-powered ZR-1 debuted in 1990 along with a new interior.

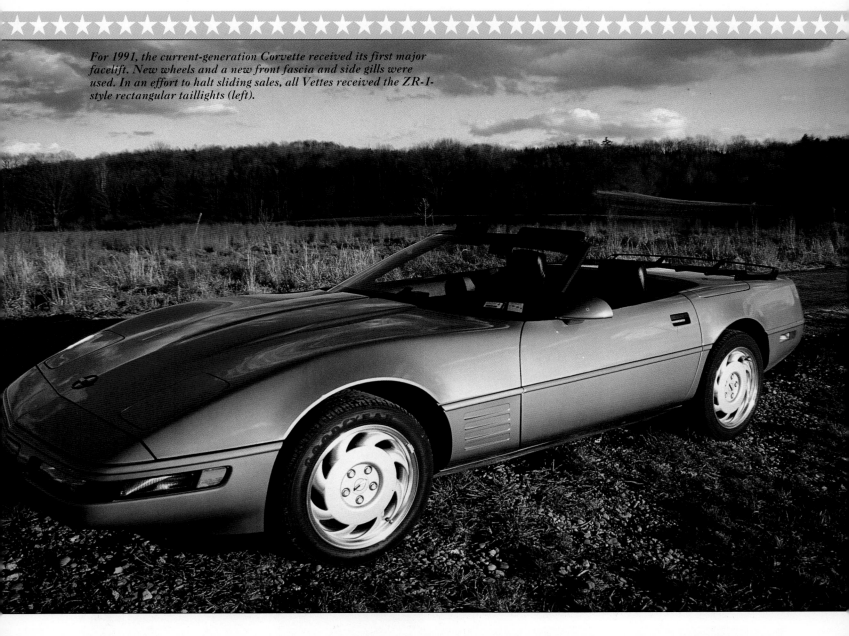

★ ★

For 1991, the current-generation Corvette received its first major facelift. New wheels and a new front fascia and side gills were used. In an effort to halt sliding sales, all Vettes received the ZR-1-style rectangular taillights (left).

were cut to feed air to the intercoolers.). Top speed was an astounding 177.9 mph and it could run low 13s in the quarter-mile. This was the supercar Americans had waited years for. A total of 121 coupes and 63 convertibles were sold that first year.

But the Callaway wasn't the only Corvette news. The standard car received a roller cam and a five-horsepower boost (to 245). Also, engineers reinforced the suspension on the coupe with some goodies they picked up from the convertible program. A new suspension option, Z-52, was introduced. It gave you better handling than the standard coupe, but without the jarring ride of the ultra-stiff Z-51. You got, among other items, the Z-51's Bilstein shocks, engine oil cooler, heavy-duty radiator and $9\frac{1}{2}$-inch wide wheels. It was available on either the coupe or the convertible and would be an option for only two years, disappearing in 1989 when the FX3 Selective Ride/Handling option debuted.

New for '88 was the introduction of 17-inch wheels as an option. Measuring $9\frac{1}{2}$ inches wide, they wore 275/40ZR

Gatorbacks. As a side bonus, the larger wheels allowed the use of 13-inch disc brakes, replacing the 11.5-inch models on the earlier cars. The larger wheels were standard on Z-51 and Z-52 models. By '89, the 17-inchers would be standard, while many other sports (or sporty) cars were still trying to fit 16-inch wheels.

The Callaway returned in 1988, this time with 382 horsepower. The ante was raised to $25,895, and a modified version of the Turbo 400 automatic was available for another $6,500. Callaway would build 25 automatics in '88 and another 18 in '89 before production halted. After that, all would be of the manual transmission variety.

Now, with 1988 being the 35th anniversary of the Corvette, you would think Chevrolet would do something special to mark the occasion. And it did. As in 1978 for the Silver Anniversary, Chevrolet offered a unique-looking model to commemorate the milestone. In '88, it was option ZO1, an all-white with black targa band paint scheme that included white wheels and a white leather interior and steering wheel. It also supplied a super

The ZR-1 has enough horsepower to melt the 315/35-series Gatorbacks right down to the cords.

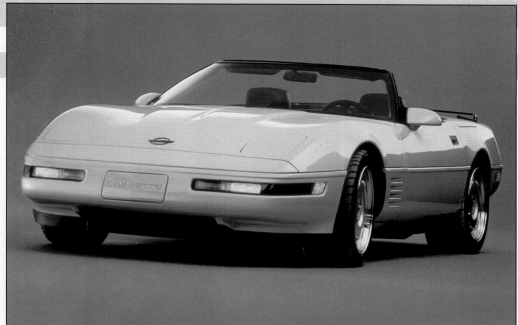

Ed Cole's small-block V8 received a redesign for 1992. Horsepower increased to 300, gas mileage went up and emissions went down. The '92s also feature a traction control system, dubbed Acceleration Slip Regulation, that works in conjunction with the anti-lock brake system.

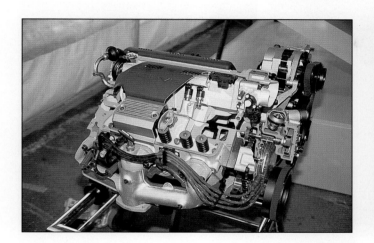

trick emblem on either side of the hood and a plaque on the console. Those who had hoped for a special performance model were disappointed.

The year 1989 was to be the Year of the King, and we don't mean Elvis. This was when the ultra-high-performance 32-valve, all-aluminum engine model was to appear. That's correct, the ZR-1. It didn't happen, but that may not have been such a bad thing. Research and development work took longer than expected, and GM wasn't about to release this motor to the public without having worked out the kinks.

While this laborious task was being attended to, Chevrolet introduced what may have been the best base Corvette ever, the 1989 model. Gone was the balky Doug Nash 4+3 transmission. In its place was a superb 6-speed built by Zahnradfabrik Friedrichshafen (ZF) in Germany. The top two gears were overdriven, with fifth being employed for top-speed runs and sixth for improved fuel economy. This, while Camaro fans couldn't order a manual transmission if they opted for the 350-cubic-inch engine.

The FX3 package, available only with the Z-51 option, gave you a choice of three suspension levels, controlled by a switch on the console. It made the Z-51 option livable on the street and made the Corvette that much more enjoyable as a sports car, especially with the new gearbox.

And while no one at Chevrolet was talking, top speed was now in the 158-160 mph range. Plus, some cars were capable of sub 14-second quarter-mile times, with 0-60 taking six seconds or sometimes less.

As almost everyone in the world now knows, the ZR-1 finally made it into production for 1990, and there may not be a more sophisticated automobile on the planet. Developed in a joint effort by Chevrolet and Lotus, here is a car that can cover the quarter-mile in under 13 seconds, go 0-60 in 4.3, top out at 180 miles per hour, plus deliver luxury and good fuel economy in the process, and still meet the government's emissions standards.

You can drive a ZR-1 flat-out on any type of race track and it won't miss a beat, or sit in stop-and-go traffic for hours on end

Callaway's latest creation in 1991, the 450-horsepower, $107,000 Speedster. Only 50 were built.

without having it overheat. This is a combination of things that none of the supercars of the Sixties could do. And perhaps only the Callaway Twin Turbo today can match it.

A new interior made it into the Corvette for the 1990 model year. It has a mix of analog and digital gauges in a high-tech package that misses the mark in many areas, such as legibility. But functionally, it is a bit of an improvement over the all-digital display.

In '91, the engine people massaged the L98 again, increasing the compression ratio one-half point to 10:1. Although the rated horsepower has not gone up, performance definitely improved. With the six-speed and 3.45:1 gears, mid-to-high 13-second quarters are there for the taking and even automatic-equipped convertibles can dip into the 13s.

For 1992, Chevrolet revised Ed Cole's venerable V8 engine. Dubbed the Generation II small-block, it features reverse-flow cooling for better thermal efficiency, a crank-triggered ignition system and a short ram fuel injection system. Not only does it produce 300 horsepower at 5000 rpm, but it is more fuel efficient and sends fewer pollutants into our fragile atmosphere. Its engine code? LT1 (now without a hyphen).

Underneath, a traction control system (called Acceleration Slip Regulation by Chevrolet) is being utilized as well. While purists may cringe, it allows the average driver to put more power to the ground safely. And it does have a disabling switch if you'd rather not use it.

What does the future hold for the Corvette? Expect more of the same. There is virtually no chance that the next generation, scheduled to appear sometime around 1995 or '96, will be the mid-engined supercar some have been expecting for the past 25 years. It will certainly be powered by a V8, at least for the first five years of the 21st century.

"People expect certain things from the Corvette," explained Dave McLellan, the marque's chief engineer since 1975. "Things like V8 power, a fiberglass body. Anything less would be a disappointment."

One thing is certain: These are good times to be a Corvette enthusiast.

Chapter Five
Show Cars, Race Cars and Future Vettes

Almost since the model's inception, the people in the Corvette group have been producing special vehicles—show cars, racers and dream machines—that have knocked the world on its collective butt. Unlike almost every other automobile on the planet, however, these one-offs and rarities almost always have given the public a glance at what the Corvette of the Future would be like. If one were to try to predict where America's flagship is headed, history dictates that it's best to look at the unusual projects going on inside General Motors.

It wasn't long after the Corvette actually hit the streets that Chevrolet was toying with it. The first of these cars appeared on the 1954 Motorama circuit. There was a roadster fitted with a hardtop, a fastback model called the Corvair and a two-door station wagon known as the Nomad. All three were stirringly beautiful. The hardtop, of course, debuted in 1956 as an option and would remain available until convertible production halted in 1975. It should have surprised no one, then, when a hardtop option was reintroduced in 1989. The only question was, "What took you so long?"

Reportedly, both the Corvair and the Nomad were considered for production. Naturally, a station wagon was not in the scheme of things and was never produced. However, many of its styling cues and the Nomad name itself were applied to a two-door wagon based on the full-sized Chevy. The '55-57 Nomads have been considered classics almost since the day the last one rolled off the assembly line, a cult favorite among hot rodders, surfers and others.

What finally killed the Corvair is still anyone's guess. Mostly, it was probably the poor sales of the production car. There's no denying its terrific looks. It became just one of many teasers that GM has thrown at the general public. On the other hand, it did foretell the day in the fall of 1962 when you would be able to purchase two very distinct types of Corvette: a convertible or a closed coupe.

If any one car embodied the styling excesses of the late '50s, it would have to be the Corvette XP-700. Designed by the late Bill Mitchell and built in the summer of 1958, it has

Sluggish sales helped kill a fastback version of the Corvette. Known as the Corvair, it was one of the stars of the '54 GM Motorama.

While Chevrolet never built a Corvette station wagon, the Nomad was actually a preview of the full-size '55 Chevy two-door wagon that would bear the same name. The 1955-57 Nomads are highly prized by hot rodders, surfers and collectors to this day.

been said (and not without a grain of truth) that it resembles an aardvark. It had a periscope for a rearview mirror, a bumble top and a host of other "Mitchellisms," most notably scoops and slats everywhere. But look closer at the rear end and you'll see the tail that appeared in 1959 on the Sting Ray racer and later on the 1961 production Vette.

Of course, as mentioned earlier in this book, the Sting Ray racer was a blatant giveaway as to what the '63 Corvette would become. True, Mitchell and Larry Shinoda probably didn't intend that to be the case. But when you pen what has gone down as the most beautiful race car in history, you don't just trash the design.

With that in mind, Mitchell and Shinoda went about shaping the Sting Ray racer into a livable street car. The finished product needs no further elaboration other than to say it is possibly the most fantastic American car ever. It is the embodiment of the Mitchell creed, which dictates that you see something new or different every time you look at it. The split window design was not an original idea; it had appeared in the '50s on both the Mercedes and on the Pegaso (not to mention the '56 Oldsmobile Golden Rocket Motorama car that Mitchell himself designed). Somehow, though, it never looked better.

Sure, the split itself was a disaster from a driver's standpoint, truly hindering rearward visibility. Mitchell and Duntov argued about it incessantly and the stylist has often drawn criticism for some of his more outlandish creations. But this was the era where form often won out over function. One only has to look at modern, look-alike automobiles to vindicate Mitchell and his work.

Soon after the 1963 Corvette was introduced, Carroll Shelby and the Ford Motor Company unleashed the Cobra on the racing world. It wasn't long—i.e., after the Cobras trounced the Vettes in their first racing appearance—before Duntov & Co. realized that their automobile, while a much better GT car, was no match for Shelby's hybrid on the track. The Cobras weighed one thousand pounds less than the new Sting Ray and had vastly superior brakes.

Zora Arkus-Duntov was not about to take this defeat lightly. Despite the AMA ban on racing, he was given the go-

Bill Mitchell's designs didn't get any stranger than the XP-700. Once you get past the obvious weirdness, however, check out the aerodynamic side mirrors (right). In one form or another, they would appear on many of Detroit's offerings over the next two decades. The tail section would show up in modified form on the Sting Ray racer in 1959 and the '61 production Corvette.

ahead from S.E. "Bunkie" Knudsen, the head of Chevrolet, to develop a Corvette lightweight to compete with the Cobra. This was the start of the Grand Sport program. The original plan was to build 125 of these racers and go fender-to-fender with Shelby.

Unfortunately, other corporate higher-ups got wind of this plan and promptly snuffed it out. General Motors' official position was still "No racing!" and that was that. The five Grand Sports were sold and raced by private parties for the next few years. While the project was aborted before the cars could become legitimate threats to the Cobras, their pedigree was undeniable with seemingly unlimited potential. How good were they?

In 1990, Chevrolet took Grand Sport No. 2 (then owned by Ed Mueller of Hawthorne, N.J.) and a new ZR-1 to compete head-to-head at Sebring. The Grand Sport was faster. Though they rarely change hands, when sold today, the lightweights command prices of more than $1 million. Not bad for a car some Chevrolet executives didn't want anything to do with.

The next important step from a styling standpoint was the original Mako Shark show car. Designed in 1962 and inspired by a predator that Mitchell caught while fishing in Bimini, this, too, had many of the styling tweaks of the '63 Corvette. More importantly, however, it really looked like a shark, right down to the gills in the front fenders. It was actually custom-painted to match Mitchell's inspiration. This car gave way (naturally) to the Mako Shark II, which (with changes) became the 1968 Corvette.

When it appeared on the show circuit in 1965, the Mako Shark II simply blew the crowds away. Its styling was so aggressive that it was almost as terrifying as a real shark. But it's important to remember that this was a time when there were very few rules. The American automobile industry was the world leader, and the competition among domestic manufacturers was fierce. Engineers and stylists could take any chance necessary to keep

The SR-2 race car.

This 1967 L88 is the only Sting Ray to ever race at the 24 Hours of Le Mans.

them ahead of the pack. Keep in mind, also, that this preceded the era of government regulation, before it cost you a million dollars in recertification money every time you changed a shape or body panel.

Once testing started on the final shape for the '68 (which was originally scheduled to debut as the 1967 model), many problems cropped up. First, you couldn't see over the high arching fenders; hence, they were shaved down a couple of inches. Second, the aerodynamics left a bit to be desired. The biggest culprit was the buildup of air under the car—especially at triple-digit speeds. To rectify the situation, a small chin spoiler was added (which also aided cooling, directing air to the radiator) and three vents were cut into each front fender behind the tire. The spoiler reduced the amount of turbulence that built up under the car and the vents helped the air escape from under the Corvette.

The third gremlin was cooling. Since the hideaway headlights blocked the grilles, there was no way at first for air to reach the radiator. It became necessary to create a path for the air. The solution was making the Corvette a bottom breather, with the necessary air being channeled in from underneath. A neat trick, and one very common on today's automobiles, more and more of which have no "traditional" grille.

When the '68 Corvette appeared in showrooms, it sold in record numbers. It was like buying a custom car without so

The Mako Shark II show car spawned the '68 Vette.

much as the expenditure for a set of aftermarket wheels. It continued to be the American dream car right up until the body style went out of production in October 1982.

Chevrolet began teasing the public with mid-engined designs back in 1960 with CERV I and the XP-819. Actually, the latter car was rear-engined, with a 327 hanging out behind the back tires. But it assuredly provided an indication of where Duntov's thinking was headed. The XP-880 (1968), XP-882 (1970) and XP-897 (1971) continued the trend, but the car that came closest to actually being the mid-engined

CERV I and II (right) were among Duntov's first mid-engined Corvette designs.

Corvette was the Four Rotor, so named because of its rotary powerplant, later to be rechristened the Aerovette after a 400-cubic-inch small-block was fitted in the engine bay.

This design may have represented Mitchell's finest hour. Indeed, he and many who worked with him believed that it was. As striking today as it was when it debuted at the Paris Auto Show in 1973, it possessed all the technological prowess that Duntov and his crew could muster. As mentioned before, this was the car that would not only move the powerplant from the front of the vehicle, but would have later incorporated all-wheel-drive technology. Its drag coefficient was 0.325—better than the 1984 production Corvette.

Alas, it wasn't to be. Strong sales, the first OPEC crunch and more than a slight case of myopia kept it out of buyers' hands. There was still a shot that the car would be produced as a 1980 model after the more traditional V8 engine was installed. But again came the decision to cancel the mid-engine program. At this point, it seems remote that such a Corvette will be built before well into the 21st century.

Still, it may be premature to write off the mid-engine design. Judging by CERV III, the idea may not be dead yet. Making its debut at the North American International Auto Show in Detroit in 1990, CERV III (which now stands for Corporate Experimental Research Vehicle, where the "C" once designated Chevrolet) features a twin-turbocharged version of the LT-5 motor that pumps out 650 horsepower and a mountain-moving 655 lbs.-ft. of torque. The engine is placed behind the driver's head and the power gets to the pavement via all four wheels.

For those not familiar with CERVs I and II, they were

The Reynolds aluminum Corvette (left) was one example of Chevy's venture into alternative body materials.

Zora Arkus-Duntov, the godfather of the Corvette, at the 1970 New York Auto Show with the XP-882 mid-engined prototype.

designed by Duntov (the first in 1960, the second in 1964). CERV I was little more than a single-seat, mid-engined competition vehicle (note the placement of the powerplant) and it had a top speed of over 200 mph. The second CERV went even further, employed full-time all-wheel-drive and hit 214 mph (the all-time speed record at the Milford Proving Grounds) with Zora himself at the controls. The technology used was nothing less than what Duntov wanted for the production Corvette.

The successor to the Corvette Indy I and II show cars of the '80s, CERV III can go 0-60 in 3.9 seconds, has a top speed of 225 mph and can pull 1.1g on the skid pad, according to Chevrolet. All this, however, is wrapped in a package that is surprisingly production-like. The interior and ergonomics are far superior to the current Vette, it has bumpers front and rear and, best of all, it actually *looks* like a Corvette. (It meets all 1990 federal safety standards.) Its drag coefficient is an exemplary 0.277.

The XP-819 (left) had a 327 hanging out behind the rear tires—strange days indeed. Bill Mitchell's Aerovette (right and above right) is considered by many to be his finest design. It was killed not once, but twice by corporate bean counters and nearsighted executives.

The brakes employ current Formula One race car technogy, using carbon-fiber rotors and carbon-fiber friction pads. All-wheel steering is part of the package to boot.

No question, this vehicle represents the high-water mark of current Corvette technology. Whether or not Chevrolet decides to abandon the front-engine, rear-drive platform when the next plasticar is produced remains to be seen. From everything this author has seen and heard, it's doubtful that it will. But that is the role of dream cars like the CERV III—to give the public something to think about, something to whet its appetite. In that regard, CERV III has a lot in common with the little white prototype that made the rounds of the 1953 Motorama circuit.

Yes, the Corvette is still the American dream car. And after almost 40 years, it remains the flagship of the fleet, the only domestically produced automobile that can not only compete with, but beat the best from around the globe.

It is the exotic American.

Corvette Indy I (left) was the progenitor of Indy II (not shown) and CERV III (above and right), the most advanced and sophisticated Corvette prototype ever.

The ZR-2 is an ongoing Chevy project. "Big doggie," as it is called, sports a 454 big-block, fuel injection and a ZF 6-speed. Chances are it will never see production, but engineers are using it to develop a kit so that late-model owners can build their own.

PHOTO CREDITS

Front Cover: Vette Magazine archives
Back Flap, top: D. Randy Riggs; bottom: Jim Campisano
Back Cover: Top: D. Randy Riggs;
middle: D. Randy Riggs; bottom: Dave Lundy
Page 6: Dave Lundy
Page 7: D. Randy Riggs
Page 8: D. Randy Riggs
Page 9: D. Randy Riggs
Page 10-11: D. Randy Riggs
Page 12-13: Jeff Bauer
Page 14-15: D. Randy Riggs
Page 16: Jim Campisano
Page 17: D. Randy Riggs
Page 18-19: Vette Magazine archives
Page 20-21: Vette Magazine archives
Page 22-23: Vette Magazine archives
Page 24-25: Jim Campisano
Page 26-27: D. Randy Riggs
Page 28-29: D. Randy Riggs
Page 30-31: D. Randy Riggs
Page 32: Vette Magazine archives
Page 33: D. Randy Riggs
Page 34-35: D. Randy Riggs
Page 36-37: Jim Campisano
Page 38-39: Jim Campisano
Page 40: Dain Gingerelli
Page 41: Jim Campisano
Page 42-43: Vette Magazine archives
Page 44-45: Dain Gingerelli
Page 46-47: Vette Magazine archives
Page 48-49: Vette Magazine archives
Page 50-51: D. Randy Riggs
Page 53: Vette Magazine archives
Page 54-55: D. Randy Riggs
Page 56-57: Vette Magazine archives
Page 58-59: D. Randy Riggs
Page 60-61: Dave Lundy
Page 62-63: Vette Magazine archives
Page 64-65: Vette Magazine archives
Page 66-67: Dave Lundy
Page 68-69: D. Randy Riggs
Page 70: Vette Magazine archives
Page 71, top: Vette magazine archives
Page 72: Jim Campisano
Page 76: Vette Magazine archives
Page 78-79: D. Randy Riggs
Page 80: Vette Magazine archives
Page 81: D. Randy Riggs
Page 82: James Resnick
Page 83: D. Randy Riggs
Page 84: D. Randy Riggs
Page 85: D. Randy Riggs
Page 90, top: Jim Campisano
Page 90, middle, bottom: Vette Magazine archives
Page 95, top: Jim Campisano

All other photos courtesy Chevrolet Motor Division